You Can Write

EXCELLENT

Reports

by Jan Fields

Consultant:
Terry Flaherty, PhD
Professor of English
Minnesota State University, Mankato

CAPSTONE PRESS
a capstone imprint

First Facts is published by Capstone Press,
1710 Roe Crest Drive, North Mankato, Minnesota 56003.
www.capstonepub.com

Books published by Capstone Press are manufactured with paper
containing at least 10 percent post-consumer waste.

Library of Congress Cataloging-in-Publication Data
Fields, Jan.
 You can write excellent reports / by Jan Fields.
  p. cm. — (First facts. You can write)
 Includes bibliographical references and index.
 Summary: "Introduces readers to the key steps in writing a school research report
through the use of examples and exercises"—Provided by publisher.
 ISBN 978-1-4296-7614-4 (library binding)
 ISBN 978-1-4296-7962-6 (paperback)
 1. Report writing—Juvenile literature. I. Title. II. Series.
 LB1047.3.F54 2012
 371.3028'1—dc23   2011035764

Editorial Credits
Jill Kalz, editor; Juliette Peters, designer; Kathy McColley, production specialist

Photo Credits
Dreamstime: Gbh007, 8, Mantonino, 19, Rmarmion, 9 (girl); Shutterstock: AnetaPics, 13, Darryl
Brooks, (12 desert scene), DM7, cover (dinosaur), 3, 12 (dinosaur), Eric Isselée, 7 (middle, right),
Eric Lam, 7 (left), Fotoline, 11, iofoto, 5, irin-k, cover (pencil), 18 (pencil), Margo Harrison,
17, matzsoca, 21, MBWTE Photos, 15, pixshots, 9 (dog), Ralf Juergen Kraft, 6, thatsmymop, 4,
Valentin Agapov, 10 (book), Vladislav Gajic, 10 (dinosaur skeleton), ZanyZeus, 18 (eraser)

Artistic Effects
Shutterstock: Roman & Olexandra (plants)

Printed in the United States of America in North Mankato, Minnesota.

102011   006405CGS12

TABLE of CONTENTS

What Is a Report?

Did you know that the heaviest dinosaur weighed more than 15 elephants? That some dinosaur teeth were 7 inches (18 centimeters) long? You can learn cool facts like these by writing a report.

Reports are a way to learn about new things. They're a way to share information. Discovering new facts can be a ton of fun!

TOPIC

Every report begins with a subject. But some subjects, such as animals, are very big. There's so much information! So pick a topic. Topics are smaller subjects within larger ones.

subject

DINOSAURS

topics

allosaurus
tyrannosaurus rex
brachiosaurus
triceratops
stegosaurus

Pick a topic you're interested in. Then write down as many questions as you can about it.

TYRANNOSAURUS REX

What did it look like?
How big was it?
What did it eat?
When and where did it live?
Did it have any enemies?

topic—what you are writing about

Time to **brainstorm**. List possible topics for a report on dogs. Choose different kinds of dogs, such as collies, poodles, or greyhounds. Then pick the dog you like best. Write down questions about it. Use the example on page 6 as a guide.

brainstorm—to come up with many ideas quickly, without stopping

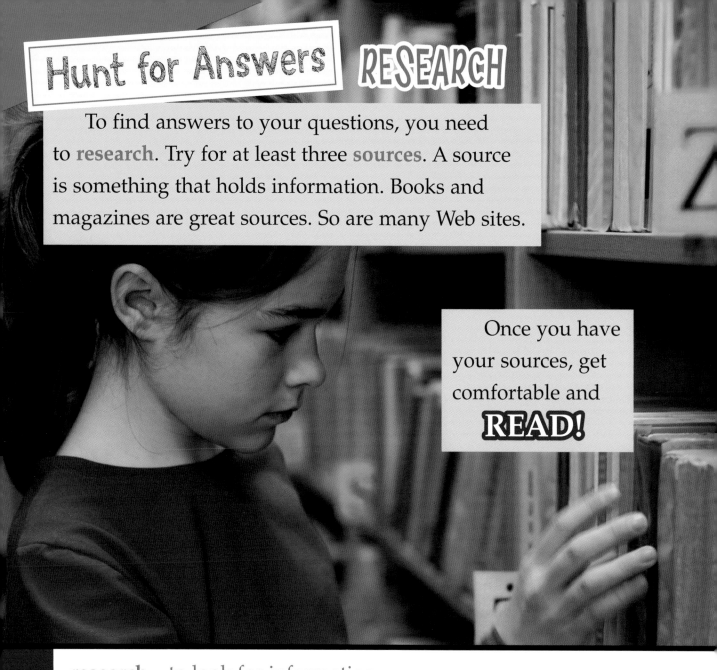

Hunt for Answers RESEARCH

To find answers to your questions, you need to **research**. Try for at least three **sources**. A source is something that holds information. Books and magazines are great sources. So are many Web sites.

Once you have your sources, get comfortable and **READ!**

research—to look for information

source—a place from which to get information

Exercise

Ask a librarian to help you look for sources about the dog you chose. Find two books and at least one magazine. Search online for more information. For example, if you chose poodles, use search words such as "poodles," "poodle facts," or "poodle information."

WRITING TIP

Not all Web sites can be trusted. Museum and college sites have good information. Sites with .org addresses are often good too. If you aren't sure, ask a librarian or your teacher. He or she will be happy to help.

TAKING NOTES

Remember what you read by writing down the facts. Note cards can help. Write a different question on the top of each card. Below, add facts that answer each question. Be sure to write down where you got each fact. Your facts are the building materials for your report.

source

For many years, museums showed tyrannosaurus rex resting on its tail. But no more! Scientists now know that T. rex stood on two feet. Its head was low. Its tail stuck out. One of its feet was raised. The dinosa... scarier tha... big and str...

WHAT DID IT LOOK LIKE? **note**

T. rex stood on two feet.

it looked scary and could run fast

(_Dangerous Dinosaurs_, page 8)

Exercise

Get a stack of index cards. Write one question from your list of dog questions on the top of each card. Then use your sources to help answer those questions. Write neatly. You need to be able to read your notes!

HOW BIG ARE POODLES?

WHAT DO POODLES EAT?

WHAT DO POODLES LIKE TO DO?

WRITING TIP

When you use book or magazine sources, include page numbers. If you need to find the information again, you'll know where to look.

Sort It Out OUTLINE

A report **outline** is like a building plan. It shows how all the parts will fit together. Facts are sorted into groups. These groups will become the paragraphs of your report. Most reports have at least three groups.

* introduction
* what T. rex looked like
* what T. rex ate
* where and when T. rex lived
* conclusion

outline—a list of a report's main points

Exercise

Sort your dog note cards into groups. Animal reports usually include how the animal looks and where it lives. You may also include how it acts and what it eats. Once you like the order of your groups, write them down. This list is your outline.

POODLES OUTLINE

introduction
size and color
what they eat
how they act
where they live
conclusion

You have the materials. You know what order to put them in. It's time to build your research report!

The **introduction** is the beginning of a report. It tells readers what the report is about. A good introduction catches readers' attention. It makes them want to read more.

One of the best-known dinosaurs is tyrannosaurus rex. It was one of the biggest meat-eaters. It could eat 500 pounds of food in one bite!

introduction

introduction—the start of a report

14

Exercise

Write an introduction for your dog report. Find a fun way to get readers interested. Try starting with a puzzle, like this example:

What dog was named for its love of water? A poodle!

WRITING TIP

Use some of your most interesting facts in the introduction. Cool facts catch readers' attention.

The Heart of It | BODY AND CONCLUSION

The **body** is the main part of a report. It holds the most important facts about the topic. The body usually has at least three paragraphs. Each paragraph starts with a topic sentence. It tells what the paragraph will be about.

topic sentences

body

T. rex was a big dinosaur. It stood about 20 feet tall and was about 40 feet long. T. rex had big legs but tiny arms.

T. rex ate meat. It had strong jaws and sharp teeth. It took huge bites of food.

T. rex lived millions of years ago. Forests were its home. All dinosaurs died 65 million years ago.

The **conclusion** ends the report. It pulls all the pieces together.

conclusion

Some dinosaurs were bigger than T. rex. But few were as terrifying!

body—the main part of a report

conclusion—the end of a report

Use your outline to write the body of your dog report. Use information from your notes. But don't just copy your notes. Write things your way. Use your own words. For the conclusion, what do you want readers to remember most about your topic?

smart!

learns tricks quickly!

lots of energy!

curly and cute!

great pets!

Fine-Tune REVISION

Revision is a big part of any kind of writing. This is your chance to proofread your report. Read it out loud. Make sure everything makes sense. You may have to add or subtract words or move things around. Check for mistakes. A report without mistakes shows you care about your work.

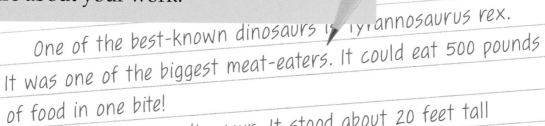

One of the best-known dinosaurs is Tyrannosaurus rex. It was one of the biggest meat-eaters. It could eat 500 pounds of food in one bite!

T. rex was a big dinosaur. It stood about 20 feet tall and was about 40 feet long. T. rex had big legs but tiny arms. T. rex ate meat. It had strong jaws and sharp teeth.

~~These bites of food.~~

~~It lived millions of years ago.~~ Forests were its home.

All dinosaurs died 65 million years ago.

Some dinosaurs were bigger than T. rex.

Few were as terrifying!

revision—the act of changing something to make it better

List Your Sources — BIBLIOGRAPHY

A **bibliography** tells where you found your facts. It lists the books, magazines, and Web sites you used. A bibliography helps readers find your sources to learn more. There are many ways to list sources. Ask your teacher for help.

book title

author name

publication year

publisher location and name

BOOKS

Cooper, Dan. Tyrannosaurus Rex. Chicago: Big Tree Books, 2010.

hnson, Jenny. Dangerous Dinosaurs. New York: Prehistoric Press, 201

page title

date viewed

site name

WEB SITE

"Fossils Everywhere." American Museum of Dinosaurs. 6 March 2012. <http://www.amdino.org/exhibitions/fossilseverywhere/.php>

address

bibliography—a list of sources

20

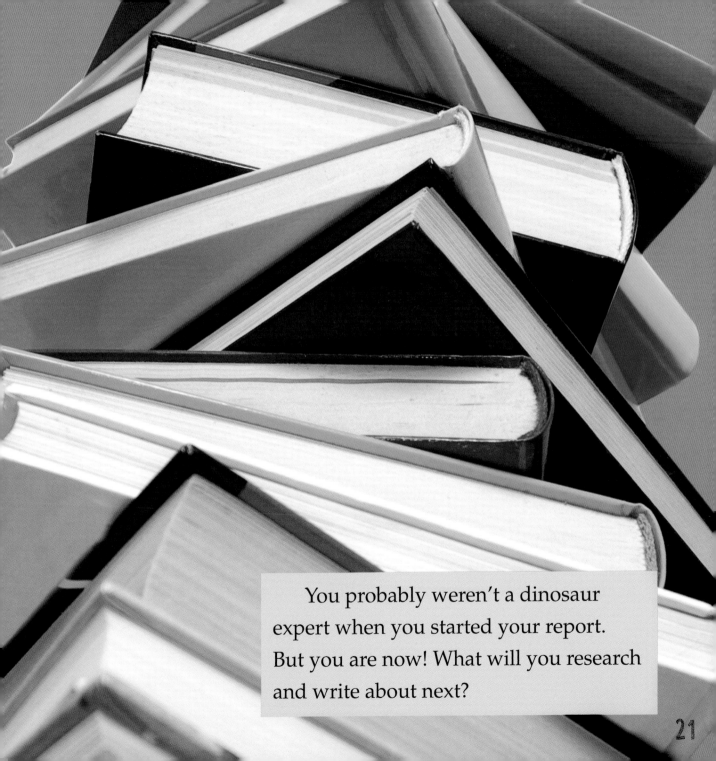

You probably weren't a dinosaur expert when you started your report. But you are now! What will you research and write about next?

Glossary

bibliography (bib-lee-OG-ruh-fee)—an alphabetical list of sources for an article or report

body (BOD-ee)—the main part of a report

brainstorm (BRAYN-storm)—coming up with lots of ideas at one time

conclusion (kuhn-KLOO-shuhn)—the ending of a report

expert (EK-spurt)—someone who knows a lot about a subject

introduction (in-truh-DUHK-shuhn)—the beginning of a report

outline (OUT-line)—a list of how facts are grouped in a report

research (REE-surch)—to study and learn about a subject

revision (ri-VIZH-uhn)—the act of changing to make better or clearer

source (SORSS)—someone or something that shares information

topic (TOP-ik)—a smaller subject within a larger one

Read More

Fandel, Jennifer. *You Can Write Awesome Stories.* You Can Write. Mankato, Minn.: Capstone Press, 2012.

Loewen, Nancy. *Just the Facts: Writing Your Own Research Report.* Writer's Toolbox. Minneapolis: Picture Window Books, 2009.

Minden, Cecilia, and Kate Roth. *How to Write a Book Report.* Language Arts Explorer Junior. Ann Arbor, Mich.: Cherry Lake Pub., 2011.

Internet Sites

FactHound offers a safe, fun way to find Internet sites related to this book. All of the sites on FactHound have been researched by our staff.

Here's all you do:

Visit *www.facthound.com*

Type in this code: 9781429676144

Super-cool stuff!

Check out projects, games and lots more at
www.capstonekids.com

23

Index